WEST MIDLANDS

LIVING MEMORIES

JULIE ROYLE was born in Cheshire and grew up there and in Northumbria. She studied history at the University of Exeter because she wanted to live in the West Country. She now lives near Worcester, in a small country cottage with a large unruly garden, and works as a freelance photographer and writer specialising in landscape, wildlife, travel, conservation, environmental issues and local history. She has a passion for Africa, which she has visited many times, but loves Britain too, particularly the English Lake District.

FRANCIS FRITH'S
PHOTOGRAPHIC MEMORIES

WEST MIDLANDS
LIVING MEMORIES

JULIE ROYLE

First published in the United Kingdom in 2003 by
Frith Book Company Ltd

Hardback Edition 2003
ISBN 1-85937-451-4

British Library Cataloguing in Publication Data

Francis Frith's West Midlands Living Memories
Julie Royle

Frith Book Company Ltd
Frith's Barn, Teffont,
Salisbury, Wiltshire SP3 5QP
Tel: +44 (0) 1722 716 376
Email: info@francisfrith.co.uk
www.francisfrith.co.uk

Printed and bound in Great Britain

Front Cover: **STOURBRIDGE**, *High Street and Public Library c1950* S213011

Frontispiece: **STOURBRIDGE**, *High Street c1950* S213033

The colour-tinting is for illustrative purposes only, and is not intended to be historically accurate

AS WITH ANY HISTORICAL DATABASE THE FRITH ARCHIVE IS CONSTANTLY
BEING CORRECTED AND IMPROVED, AND THE PUBLISHERS WOULD
WELCOME INFORMATION ON OMISSIONS OR INACCURACIES

CONTENTS

FRANCIS FRITH
VICTORIAN PIONEER

FRANCIS FRITH, founder of the world-famous photographic archive, was a complex and multi-talented man. A devout Quaker and a highly successful Victorian businessman, he was philosophic by nature and pioneering in outlook.

By 1855 he had already established a wholesale grocery business in Liverpool, and sold it for the astonishing sum of £200,000, which is the equivalent today of over £15,000,000. Now a very rich man, he was able to indulge his passion for travel. As a child he had pored over travel books written by early explorers, and his fancy and imagination had been stirred by family holidays to the sublime mountain regions of Wales and Scotland. 'What lands of spirit-stirring and enriching scenes and places!' he had written. He was to return to these scenes of grandeur in later years to 'recapture the thousands of vivid and tender memories', but with a different purpose. Now in his thirties, and captivated by the new science of photography, Frith set out on a series of pioneering journeys up the Nile and to the Near East that occupied him from 1856 unti 1860.

INTRIGUE AND EXPLORATION

These far-flung journeys were packed with intrigue and adventure. In his life story, written when he was sixty-three, Frith tells of being held captive by bandits, and of fighting 'an awful midnight battle to the very point of surrender with a deadly pack of hungry, wild dogs'. Wearing flowing Arab costume, Frith arrived at Akaba by camel seventy years before Lawrence of Arabia, where he encountered 'desert princes and rival sheikhs, blazing with jewel-hilted swords'.

He was the first photographer to venture beyond the sixth cataract of the Nile. Africa was still the mysterious 'Dark Continent', and Stanley and Livingstone's historic meeting was a decade into the future. The conditions for picture taking confound belief. He laboured for hours in his wicker dark-room in the sweltering heat of the desert, while the volatile chemicals fizzed dangerously in their trays. Back in London he exhibited his photographs and was 'rapturously cheered' by members of the Royal Society. His reputation as a photographer was made overnight.

VENTURE OF A LIFE-TIME

Characteristically, Frith quickly spotted the opportunity to create a new business as a specialist publisher of photographs. He lived in an era of immense and sometimes violent change. For the poor, in the early part of Victoria's reign, work was exhausting and the hours long, and people had precious little free time to enjoy themselves. Most people had no transport other than a cart or gig at their disposal, and rarely

business one only has to look at the catalogue issued by Frith & Co in 1886: it runs to some 670 pages, listing not only many thousands of views of the British Isles but also many photographs of most European countries, and China, Japan, the USA and Canada - note the sample page shown here from the hand-written Frith & Co ledgers recording the pictures. By 1890 Frith had created the greatest specialist photographic publishing company in the world, with over 2,000 sales outlets - more than the combined number that Boots and WH Smith have today! The picture on page 9 shows the Frith & Co display board at Ingleton in the Yorkshire Dales (left of window). Beautifully constructed with a mahogany frame and gilt inserts, it could display up to a dozen local scenes.

POSTCARD BONANZA

The ever-popular holiday postcard we know today took many years to develop. In 1870 the Post Office issued the first plain cards, with a pre-printed stamp on one face. In 1894 they allowed other publishers' cards to be sent through the mail with an attached adhesive halfpenny stamp. Demand grew rapidly, and in 1895 a new size of postcard was permitted called the court card, but there was little room for illustration. In 1899, a year after Frith's death, a new card measuring 5.5 x 3.5 inches became the standard format, but it was not until 1902 that the divided back came into being, so that the address and message could be on one face and a full-size illustration on the other. Frith & Co were in the vanguard of postcard development: Frith's sons Eustace and Cyril continued their father's monumental task, expanding the number of views offered to the public and recording more and more places in Britain, as the coasts and countryside were opened up to mass travel.

Francis Frith had died in 1898 at his villa in Cannes, his great project still growing. The archive he created continued in business for another seventy years. By 1970 it contained over a third of a million pictures showing 7,000 British towns and villages.

travelled far beyond the boundaries of their own town or village. However, by the 1870s the railways had threaded their way across the country, and Bank Holidays and half-day Saturdays had been made obligatory by Act of Parliament. All of a sudden the working man and his family were able to enjoy days out and see a little more of the world.

With typical business acumen, Francis Frith foresaw that these new tourists would enjoy having souvenirs to commemorate their days out. In 1860 he married Mary Ann Rosling and set out on a new career: his aim was to photograph every city, town and village in Britain. For the next thirty years he travelled the country by train and by pony and trap, producing fine photographs of seaside resorts and beauty spots that were keenly bought by millions of Victorians. These prints were painstakingly pasted into family albums and pored over during the dark nights of winter, rekindling precious memories of summer excursions.

THE RISE OF FRITH & CO

Frith's studio was soon supplying retail shops all over the country. To meet the demand he gathered about him a small team of photographers, and published the work of independent artist-photographers of the calibre of Roger Fenton and Francis Bedford. In order to gain some understanding of the scale of Frith's

FRANCIS FRITH'S LEGACY

Frith's legacy to us today is of immense significance and value, for the magnificent archive of evocative photographs he created provides a unique record of change in the cities, towns and villages throughout Britain over a century and more. Frith and his fellow studio photographers revisited locations many times down the years to update their views, compiling for us an enthralling and colourful pageant of British life and character.

We are fortunate that Frith was dedicated to recording the minutiae of everyday life. For it is this sheer wealth of visual data, the painstaking chronicle of changes in dress, transport, street layouts, buildings, housing, engineering and landscape that captivates us so much today. His remarkable images offer us a powerful link with the past and with the lives of our ancestors.

THE VALUE OF THE ARCHIVE TODAY

Computers have now made it possible for Frith's many thousands of images to be accessed almost instantly. Frith's images are increasingly used as visual resources, by social historians, by researchers into genealogy and ancestry, by architects and town planners, and by teachers involved in local history projects.

In addition, the archive offers every one of us an opportunity to examine the places where we and our families have lived and worked down the years. Highly successful in Frith's own era, the archive is now, a century and more on, entering a new phase of popularity. Historians consider the Francis Frith Collection to be of prime national importance. It is the only archive of its kind remaining in private ownership. Francis Frith's archive is now housed in an historic timber barn in the beautiful village of Teffont in Wiltshire. Its founder would not recognize the archive office as it is today. In place of the many thousands of dusty boxes containing glass plate negatives and an all-pervading odour of photographic chemicals, there are now ranks of computer screens. He would be amazed to watch his images travelling round the world at unimaginable speeds through internet lines.

The archive's future is both bright and exciting. Francis Frith, with his unshakeable belief in making photographs available to the greatest number of people, would undoubtedly approve of what is being done today with his lifetime's work. His photographs depicting our shared past are now bringing pleasure and enlightenment to millions around the world a century and more after his death.

WEST MIDLANDS
AN INTRODUCTION

OUR county system evolved more than 1,000 years ago, and it has helped to engender strong local loyalties. If several generations of your family have lived in Staffordshire, for instance, the chances are that you feel yourself to be a Staffordian through and through, with a deep affection for the county of your birth. Of course, boundaries have never been sacrosanct, and many small changes did occur over the centuries for one reason or another. There have always been plenty of anomalies too. Take Dudley, for instance: though geographically in Staffordshire, and surrounded on all sides by Staffordshire, it was for a long time an 'island' of Worcestershire. Nonetheless, anomalies and alterations were generally small enough to be absorbed without too much upset. In the 1970s, however, the government set about a reorganisation which was to change the county map radically. This was laid down in the Local Government Act 1972, which

HARBORNE, *Prince's Corner and High Street c1955* H365014

came into force in 1974 to almost universal disapproval. It might have been acceptable had it simply been a question of small-scale rationalisation where this seemed desirable. After all, no one could claim that all our boundaries were logical. But it was much more than rationalisation; it was a process which, with little regard for history, tradition, local identity or sense of community, wrenched huge chunks from unwilling counties and presented them to their neighbours. Or, even worse, it cobbled together these stolen territories with others to form completely new counties - as if one could simply invent a county.

West Midlands was one of the most unpopular creations of the Act. For a start, the very name was confusing. We already had a West Midlands; it was that region which most people took to encompass Staffordshire, Shropshire, Worcestershire, Herefordshire and Warwickshire. The new county of West Midlands, however, merely comprised parts of Staffordshire, Worcestershire and Warwickshire. Worcestershire lost comparatively little to this upstart creation, and in any case there were plenty who were snobbishly glad to be rid of Stourbridge and Halesowen, even if the residents of those towns were not so pleased. But if Worcestershire got off lightly, Staffordshire and Warwickshire did not. At a stroke of the bureaucrat's pen, Staffordshire lost around half its population: 900,000 people, many of them living in Wolverhampton, a large, independently minded town fiercely proud of its heritage. Warwickshire lost even more, not only Birmingham, but also long-established boroughs like Sutton Coldfield and Solihull, which had managed to retain something of their own identity even while inevitably becoming Birmingham suburbs. And Coventry was taken too, even though it was a completely separate city with a heritage distinctly its own. But Coventry was perceived as an industrial town, and industry was what this new West Midlands was all about. Warwickshire became an almost wholly rural county and lost 1.5 million people, three-quarters of its population.

Was it a bad idea then, this new county? Most people thought so. But then again, perhaps it is not that simple. We have such a mobile society these days that not so many of us do still live in the place inhabited by generations of our forebears. And perhaps a Brummie's first loyalty is to Birmingham, not to Warwickshire, and a Wulfrunian's to Wolverhampton, rather than Staffordshire. And let us not forget that the Black Country, which is seen by many as a distinct entity, was formerly split between two counties. So is it reasonable to get too upset about the creation of a county called West Midlands? Isn't it just another meaningless label? Does it really matter? Perhaps boundaries are not only insignificant, but also divisive. Perhaps they are barriers, and we should be trying to break them down.

People complain that the creation of West Midlands lumped together folk with different traditions, loyalties, attitudes and accents - but is that so awful? Isn't that what multiculturalism is all about? Many of the county's residents are of immigrant stock, recent or otherwise. The region has always been open to immigration, both from the rest of the British Isles and from abroad. It was French Huguenots who established the glass-making industry in 17th-century Stourbridge. More recently, it was Kashmiris who made Birmingham famous for its superb Balti restaurants.

Whatever the differences between the communities that make up the county, there are also certain unifying themes which may be more significant. Industry is the most obvious one, but change is another, while the people, whatever their origins, have always been remarkable for adaptability, inventiveness and initiative. The area is best known for metal working and heavy manufacturing industries, but that is just a tiny part of the story. In reality, the towns and cities of West Midlands have been involved in just about every activity known to man. Agriculture dominated their early history, and the first industries to develop were linked to farming. Large-scale production in manufacturing industries became possible only after the move towards mechanisation in the 18th century. By the late 20th century, heavy industry was already in decline, while service industries and information technology were growing in importance. West Midlanders had to adapt, and they did. When Bilston Steelworks closed in 1979, that Black Country town lost its largest employer, but it survived. Its people had applied their skills to a variety of trades in the past; they would do so again. When Round Oak Steelworks at Brierley Hill closed in the early 1980s, another Black Country town was devastated. But its inhabitants did not sit in the pub whingeing. The site was soon cleared, and the massive Merry Hill shopping and leisure complex was constructed, providing new employment. It is still going strong - on 27 December 2001, the BBC reported that an estimated 120,000 shoppers had occupied the day spending their Christmas money (or returning unwanted presents) at Merry Hill (or Merry Hell, as it is known to the unconverted).

All the larger towns and cities of West Midlands have long been involved in a multitude of different trades and industries. Birmingham grew rich as an agricultural market town which also made farm implements. By Tudor times it was famous for both its cattle markets and its blacksmiths. It was only in the 17th century that it became clear that the future lay predominantly in metal. The farm tool trade developed into specialised blade making, and then blades gave way to guns. At the same time, though, Birmingham was working at just about every other industry and activity you could think of, eventually earning itself such titles as 'city of a thousand trades' and 'workshop of the world'. Even today, everything from chocolate to wedding rings to motor cars is still made in Birmingham.

Coventry was for a long time the world's biggest car maker, and many people associate it with nothing else. Its first motor car was produced in 1898, and cars are still made there today. But Coventry was also once the world's biggest bicycle maker. And long before that, in the days when it was the fourth most important English town (well ahead of Birmingham for many centuries), Coventry dealt primarily in wool and textile manufacture. Earl Leofric and Countess Godiva laid the foundations for this when they established a Benedictine monastery in 1043. The land they gave to the monks was used for raising sheep, the first step in a process which was to make Coventry the centre of the cloth-weaving industry for nearly 500 years. Leather production was important in the early days too, and so was needle making. When 19th-century mechanisation made it possible, Coventry progressed from making needles to making sewing machines.

Wolverhampton, 'capital of the Black Country', was a late starter compared to its larger neighbours, but it grew rich on the wool trade in the 14th and 15th centuries. After that, trade declined. Wolverhampton continued to prosper in a quiet way as a country market town, but it was only in the 18th century that industry began to take root. Before long it had diversified into so many trades - everything from brewing to japanning - that it was for a long time effectively recession-proof. Between 1801 and 1901 its population rose from 12,500 to 95,000, but not until 2001 did Wolverhampton succeed in its bid to become a city.

The smaller Black Country towns are a diverse bunch. Some were established as market towns early in the Middle Ages, while others barely existed until the 18th century. Some were involved in coal mining from the 1300s onwards, but none was involved in large-scale industrialisation before the late 18th century. Each participated in a variety of trades, but each also had its own speciality: Walsall made saddles and other equine goods, Cradley made chains, Willenhall made locks, Darlaston made nuts and bolts, Wednesfield made traps, and Stourbridge and its neighbours made glass. This diversity meant that in times of recession the region as a whole had more resilience than most, though individual towns might suffer.

Things have never been static here. In the early days of industrialisation, green fields became 'dark satanic mills' almost overnight, and the region became the industrial heartland of the world. There has been constant renewal ever since. As craft industries gave way to mechanisation and mass production, small forges, furnaces and workshops were replaced by large brick factories which were later replaced by prefabricated sheds. As the population increased, cottages were replaced by terraces which were replaced by enormous estates and tower blocks. As transport assumed more and more importance, pot-holed roads were sidelined by canals which were superseded by railways which were too often replaced by dual carriageways and motorways. Now the latest twist has canals and former industrial premises being spruced up for a new generation of leisure users, while collieries and quarries are turned into parks and nature reserves, and former railways into walkways and cycleways. There is much talk about the 'greening of the Black Country', and huge swathes of the county are bristling with ambitious regeneration projects. New building is everywhere, most of it fortunately of a higher standard than we have seen for

MOSELEY, *The Lake, Chantry Park c1965* M154007

many years - nobody wants to repeat the mistakes of the 1950s-60s. The new bus station and new art gallery in Walsall are just two recent buildings which have received national acclaim, while Birmingham city centre is currently undergoing yet another of the massive transformations which are periodically undertaken. It looks as though this might be the one which really will turn Brum into the world-class city it already believes itself to be.

We have already discussed how the West Midlands county created in 1974 was not popular. Just as people were beginning to get used to the idea, further administrative changes were brought about. The county council was replaced by a clutch of what the bureaucrats call 'unitary authorities', such as Dudley Metropolitan Borough. In deciding how to divide this book into chapters, I have made use of the administrative boundaries, purely for practical reasons. The first chapter is devoted to Birmingham suburbs (there are no relatively recent photographs of the city centre in the Frith archive) and the second to Solihull and a selection of its suburbs. It should be noted here that Solihull is not just a suburb of Birmingham, for it retains a certain independence as a metropolitan borough. Places such as Olton and Shirley are administratively within that borough, not within the City of Birmingham. Coventry gets a chapter to itself, of course, but it was more difficult to work out how to apportion the Black Country towns. Eventually, I decided to go for a north-south divide. The northern section includes Walsall, with some of its suburbs, and some Wolverhampton suburbs, though there are no photographs of the city centre. The southern section is taken up entirely by the borough of Dudley, so that it includes places as diverse as Old Swinford and West Bromwich, which are nonetheless geographically close and administratively linked.

BRIERLEY HILL, *The Canal Locks c1965* B355005

BIRMINGHAM
THE SUBURBS

EDGBASTON, *Queen Elizabeth Hospital c1955* E85007

Designed by Lanchester and Lodge, who were appointed after winning a competition in 1930, this was originally known as the Birmingham Hospitals Centre at Edgbaston; it was later named after Queen Elizabeth, the late Queen Mother. Construction began in the early 1930s on land donated by the Cadbury family, and the first patients were admitted in 1937.

HARBORNE
High Street c1965
H365027

Originally in Staffordshire, Harborne was taken into Birmingham in 1891. It had already been popular with wealthy city merchants for a century or so, and much housing development had taken place along the High Street. Today, Harborne remains a largely residential suburb, with a great diversity of housing. Prominent residents have included the poet W H Auden and the artist David Cox.

HARBORNE
The Bell Inn c1955
H365019

The Bell occupies a pleasant site, almost semi-rural in character, tucked away on Old Church Road, with the sandstone tower of St Peter's as a backdrop, and Victorian houses nearby. It is Harborne's oldest pub, at least 300 years old; fortunately it looks much the same today as in 1955, except that its windows have acquired some kitsch bull's-eye glass.

HARBORNE, *The Boys' House, Birmingham Blue Coat School c1955* H365001

The first Blue Coat School opened in central Birmingham in 1724. It was a charity school whose pupils wore blue coats. When the school outgrew its site, land was purchased at Harborne in 1913 to build a bigger school, but it was 1930 before it opened. In 1960 it became an independent prep school for day pupils and boarders.

HARBORNE
The Green Man c1965
H365028

The Green Man is a common pub name (and church carving), deriving from an ancient fertility figure, though his exact significance is uncertain. He is usually depicted with foliage issuing from his mouth, or sprouting from his head like hair. M&B's Green Man, however, is a green-jacketed character with a gun and a hunting dog.

HARBORNE, *Prince's Corner c1965* H365042

This splendid building is less impressive today. The upper floors have an air of neglect, while George Mason's has been replaced by a modern shopfront proclaiming www.designerchildrenswear.com. Prince's Corner was named after Prince Albert - as if to emphasise the point, the road on the left here is Albert Road.

► **HARBORNE**
*Prince's Corner and
High Street c1955*
H365014

Here we have another
view of Prince's Corner
on the right, with a
glimpse of the High
Street beyond the
pseudo-timbering of
The King's Arms (now
The Fallow and Firkin).
When the roundabout
was built in the 1930s, it
was deemed such a
novelty that it starred
on specially issued local
postcards, the
handsome buildings in
the background playing
only a minor role.

◄ **HARBORNE**
The Duke of York c1955
H365013

Hardly changed today,
this substantial, good-
looking pub still stands
opposite Prince's Corner
at the end of the High
Street. This spot has
been the terminus and
turning point for buses
from Birmingham city
centre since the very
first motor buses to
serve Harborne
departed the city in
1903, travelling (as they
still do) via Five Ways
and Edgbaston.

▲ **NORTHFIELD,** *Bristol Road South c1955* N203006

Northfield was founded by Saxon settlers in the fertile valley of the River Rea. The original village remained agricultural, but a subsidiary settlement grew up on the Bristol road which had already become a sizeable suburb when Northfield was incorporated into Birmingham in 1911. The last farm in the parish survived until the 1960s, a few years after this view was taken.

◄ **NORTHFIELD**
Bristol Road South c1955
N203008

The catalyst for the subsidiary settlement mentioned in the caption to N203006 was the building of two turnpike roads through Northfield, one of which was eventually to become the A38 (Bristol Road). A large coaching inn called The Bell was built at their intersection. The Bell crossing remains an important hub today, and development is still concentrated along Bristol Road.

NORTHFIELD, *The Parish Church c1955* N203004

Northfield is frequently described as having retained much of its village character. This is optimistic, to say the least, but the heart of the former village is still a pleasant and rather unexpected scene of brick cottages, a pub, a former cattle pound and this sandstone church. Dedicated to St Laurence, the church was built in the 12th century but has been much altered since.

NORTHFIELD
The Black Horse c1955
N203007

The mock-Tudor style is often mocked, but anybody taking the Bristol Road through Northfield today (and possibly even in 1955) would struggle to find a better-looking building than this mock-Tudor pub, designed by C E Bateman for Davenport's brewery and completed in 1929. It is one of the finest examples of its type.

THE LICKEY HILLS *c1965* L215368

The Lickey Hills were declared a royal hunting forest in the 11th century, but they were sold by the Crown to the Earl of Plymouth in 1682. They were acquired by Birmingham Corporation through purchase and donation between the 1880s and the 1920s, and opened to the public. The Lickeys attract 500,000 visitors a year, some of whom climb Beacon Hill (975ft) to enjoy a view said to encompass 10 counties.

▼ **THE LICKEY HILLS,** *Four Ways c1955* L215315

The Lickey Hills are actually in Worcestershire, and so is this road junction, though only just. As the hills are owned by Birmingham, it is reasonable to include the area in this book. This photograph shows Bilberry Hill, and was taken from Groveley Lane, which meets Lickey Road, Barnt Green Road and Rose Hill at the junction traditionally known as Four Ways.

▼ **LICKEY HILLS,** *Four Ways c1965* L215367

The mock-Tudor Chalet Club in this view is now The Poacher's Pocket, a busy pub. People mostly arrive at the Lickeys by car today (though there are plenty of buses), but from 1913 to 1924 they came by bus, and from 1924 to 1952 on the hugely popular Number 70 tram, which served nearby Rednal Terminus on Lickey Road.

▶ **LICKEY HILLS,** *Four Ways c1955* L215317

Pictures taken of Four Ways in the 1920s reveal a delightful rural scene. Only 30 years later, it has become just another branch of suburbia. Some picturesque cottages were destroyed to widen these roads and create the roundabout, which now dominates the view. On the far side of the roundabout is Lickey Road, the main route from Birmingham.

25

▼ **LICKEY HILLS,** *The Cofton Wood Tea Room c1955* L215340D

In the 1920s, when the Lickeys were at the height of their popularity, several tea rooms were in business, and this one was still going strong in the 1950s. The proprietor, F York Jones, used to advertise proudly that Cofton Wood Tea Room had 'special arrangements for supplying jugs of tea without waiting, even on the busiest days.'

► **LICKEY HILLS**
The Cofton Wood Pleasure Grounds c1955 L215340A

The miniature railway at Cofton Wood was nearly as popular as the tea room, though one cannot help wondering if the adults in this picture are not just the teeniest bit embarrassed. Another highlight for children used to be the travelling fair which visited the Lickeys on bank holidays, occupying a site on the corner of Lickey Road and Leach Green Lane.

◄ KING'S NORTON

The Old Saracen's Head Inn c1960 K83006

A painted inscription on the wall claims that The Saracen's Head was built in the 11th century. However, the present building dates mainly from the 15th century. Since then it has served as an inn, a grocer's shop, a chemist's, a tea room, a community centre and a royal bailiff's residence. It is the parish office today, and is in need of some restoration.

► KING'S NORTON

The Village Green c1960 K83003

Formerly in Worcestershire, King's Norton became part of Birmingham in 1911. It remains one of the leafier suburbs, though in 1936 the city council destroyed much of its appeal by demolishing the lovely old cottages which clustered round the green. Three fine buildings remain, however: St Nicholas' church, the Old Saracen's Head and the Old Grammar School.

▼ **KING'S NORTON,** *The Park c1960* K83014

In the 16th century John Leland described King's Norton as 'a pretty uplandish town in Worcs ... good plenty of wood and pasture ...' The woods and pasture have gone, but some greenery remains. In this picture the 15th-century spire of St Nicholas's church overlooks the park, which incorporates the tree-lined drive to the former vicarage, demolished in 1970.

► **KING'S NORTON,** *The Old Grammar School c1960* K83010

This is one of the oldest schools in the Midlands. The timber-framed upper storey, supported on pillars, was built in the 15th century; the ground floor was underbuilt in the Elizabethan period. Its most famous schoolmaster was the Presbyterian preacher Thomas Hall, who presided from 1629 to 1667 and wrote stern pamphlets on such subjects as 'The loathsomeness of long hair.'

MOSELEY
St Mary's Row c1965
M154006

In the mid 19th century, as Birmingham expanded rapidly, wealthy businessmen were moving out of the city to prime suburbs such as Edgbaston, Harborne and Moseley, where some large, imposing residences sprang up. Towards the end of the century many smaller houses were also built in Moseley, which became a notably cosmopolitan community.

▶ **MOSELEY**
The Green c1965
M154001

This must be one of the smallest and one of the most recently created greens in the country. The road past St Mary's church originally took an indirect course to avoid a marshy area, but in 1801 the marsh was drained and a more direct road was built. The tiny triangle of land between the old and new roads became the green.

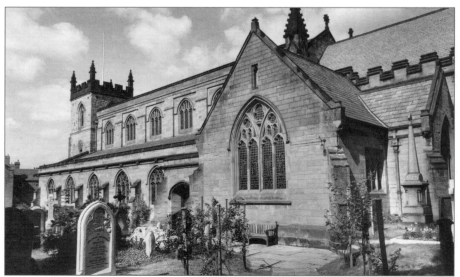

◀ **MOSELEY**
St Mary's Church c1955
M154003

Moseley's inhabitants originally had to travel to King's Norton for church services, but at some time in the 15th century they acquired a chapel. A tower was added in 1513. St Mary's was rebuilt in 1780. It was further altered and extended on several occasions, notably by Thomas Rickman in 1823-24, J A Chatwin in 1886 and 1897 and P B Chatwin in 1910 and 1940.

▲ **MOSELEY,** *The Lake, Chantry Park c1965* M154007

Moseley Hall was the medieval home of the Grevis family, but in 1891 the hall and its surrounding parkland became the property of the city. In 1896 Salisbury Road was constructed, bisecting Moseley Hall Park. The northern part was bought by a consortium of businessmen who built houses overlooking it. Chantry Park is known as Moseley Park today, and is accessible only to keyholders.

◄ **ACOCK'S GREEN**
Shaftmoor Lane c1955
A136040

Pictures of Shaftmoor Lane taken around 1900 show a delightful country lane bordered by trees and hedges. Some trees remain, but the lane would no longer be recognisable to someone who knew it in those days. It takes its name from 16th-century Shaftmoor Farm, which was demolished in 1929 soon after the estate had been sold to Birmingham Corporation.

ACOCK'S GREEN
Olton Boulevard East
c1965 A136028

Olton Boulevard East is a long, wide road of mostly municipal housing, linking Warwick Road with Shaftmoor Lane. At its western end, between Shaftmoor Lane and Fox Hollies Road, there is a parade of early 20th-century shops, and opposite there is a late 20th-century supermarket. The parade still looks much like this today, and the end shop is still Shaftmoor Lane Post Office.

ACOCK'S GREEN, *Olton Boulevard East c1965* A136035

This view of the parade is taken from the junction with Fox Hollies Road, at the opposite end to photograph No A136028. George Mason's (the first of the mock-Tudor buildings) is now a Spar, but essentially little has changed since 1965, except that traffic would dominate any picture taken today. A modern supermarket now stands on the right (behind the bus).

ACOCK'S GREEN
Olton Boulevard East
c1955 A136043

Here we have another view of the shopping parade, looking west towards Shaftmoor Lane. This part of Acock's Green is known as 'the village', but the centre of the community is further east, nearer the railway station, which opened in 1852. This gave a major boost to development, though it was not until the 1920s that building really became intense.

ACOCK'S GREEN, *The Roundabout, Olton Boulevard East c1955* A136041

It is strange to think that until the 1830s Acock's Green was a rural village. In 1839 the estate was sold to developers, but it was 1911 before it became part of Birmingham. Olton Boulevard East was created from former country lanes in 1928, to serve a vast municipal housing estate reckoned to be a model of its kind.

ACOCK'S GREEN, *Clifton House c1965* A136021

Clifton House occupies the corner of Fox Hollies Road and
Olton Boulevard East, and had probably been only recently
completed when the photograph was taken. It remains
unchanged today, but the shapely elm tree in the background
has gone, presumably a victim of Dutch elm disease. However,
the spindly cherry trees on the roundabout look a lot more
substantial now.

ACOCK'S GREEN
Hall Green,
Pemberley Road c1965
A136023

These are Coppice House, Hollypiece House and Homemeadow House, named after fields on the Fox Hollies estate. The flats occupy the site of Zaccheus Walker's mansion, The Hollies. It was approached through an avenue of trees, which still stand on Greenwood Avenue, while only a gate pillar, and the base of another, remain of the entrance to the long-demolished hall.

ACOCK'S GREEN, *Fox Hollies Road c1955* A136042

A farm called Atte Hollies was recorded in 1275 in what later became Hall Green. By 1626 it had been acquired by the Fox family, and was known as Foxholleys. It subsequently belonged to Zaccheus Walker, who rebuilt the house in grand style, calling it The Hollies. It was the most imposing mansion in the neighbourhood, but it was demolished in 1937.

▼ **YARDLEY,** *Blakesley Hall c1965* Y18001

Until incorporated into Birmingham in 1911, Yardley had been a rural Worcestershire manor for nearly 1,000 years, but only the church and a couple of timber-framed buildings survive from those days. This is one of them, a beautiful Elizabethan property rebuilt on the site of an earlier moated house by prosperous merchant Richard Smallbroke in 1575.

► **YARDLEY**

Bakeman House c1965
Y18011

This is part of the Tivoli Centre on Coventry Road. Erected in the 1960s, it neatly sums up the building trends of the time. Aggregates and cladding panels have been used extensively on the tower block; with its associated shopping precinct and multi-storey car park, it overlooks an underpass and a flyover on the outer ring road.

◄ **YARDLEY**
The Yew Tree c1965
Y18010

The Yew Tree was built in 1925 in the grounds of Yardley House on Yew Tree Lane. Yardley House had belonged to prominent local families such as the Minshulls and the Flavells, but in 1919 the Flavells sold the house to the brewers Mitchells & Butlers, who built the pub and then demolished Yardley House in 1930.

▶ **CASTLE BROMWICH**
The Green c1965 C281004

There was a settlement on this site in prehistoric times, but the first documentary reference to 'Bramwice' was in 1168. The name referred to the wild broom which grew here. The castle was on a hill north of the church, comprising a motte and bailey with earth and timber fortifications. Though just a Birmingham suburb now, Castle Bromwich retains its green and a few old houses.

CASTLE BROMWICH
Hurst Lane c1965
C281013

From the late 19th century the agricultural estates of Castle Bromwich were sold off for house building to accommodate overspill. The 1930s was the start of the biggest housing boom, which continued intermittently until the 1980s, when the last farmland was sold. Hurst Lane leads to Shard End Estate, the land for which was bought by compulsory purchase order in 1945.

SUTTON COLDFIELD, *Birmingham Road c1965* S339082

Sutton Coldfield initially grew in linear fashion along the Birmingham-Lichfield road. It retained its predominantly rural character until industry began to develop in the 17th and 18th centuries. Mills were built to harness the abundant local water supplies, but when steam power took over from water power, Sutton's industrial life waned; today it is mainly residential.

SUTTON COLDFIELD
*The Boddington Garden
c1960* S339032

Dr Boddington was a local man; in 1840 he wrote a pioneering paper on the treatment of TB, then known as pulmonary consumption. He advocated open-air treatment and successfully put his ideas into practice in his sanatorium (demolished in 1935) at Maney. He saved numerous lives before the advent of modern drugs revolutionised the treatment of the disease.

SUTTON COLDFIELD, *Birmingham Road c1965* S339084

Sutton has one great asset which makes it a cut above other Birmingham suburbs - Sutton Park, which was given to the town by Henry VIII at the behest of local benefactor Bishop John Vesey. The bishop also set up schemes for the unemployed, paved the streets, built 50 cottages, endowed a boys' grammar school and financed extensions to the church.

▼ **SUTTON COLDFIELD,** *The Boddington Garden and Beeches Walk c1965* S339076

Though Dr Boddington was most famous for his work with TB patients, he also cared for mentally ill patients at Driffold House Asylum at the corner of Wyndley Lane and The Driffold. In 1953 this garden, at the junction of Birmingham Road and The Driffold, was remodelled and named in Dr Boddington's honour.

▶ **SUTTON COLDFIELD**
Wyndley Pool, Sutton Park c1960
S339057

During the reign of Henry V (1413-22), several pools were constructed, probably for the Earl of Warwick, in what was later to become Sutton Park. Wyndley Pool was almost certainly one of them. There used to be a 17th-century water mill by the pool, but it was demolished in 1962, soon after this photograph was taken.

◀ **SUTTON COLDFIELD**
Bracebridge Pool,
Sutton Park c1960
S339301

With 2,500 acres of heathland, ancient woodland and wetland, Sutton Park constitutes the finest countryside in the county. While it is of great importance for wildlife, it is also immensely valuable for human recreation. It has been used for that purpose since the time of the Anglo-Saxon kingdom of Mercia, though they went hunting in those days, not angling.

▶ **SUTTON COLDSFIELD**
Bracebridge Pool,
Sutton Park c1955
S339022

Bracebridge Pool was formed around 1420 and leased to Sir Ralph Bracebridge at a yearly rent of £10 or 120 bream. In 1921 a catering business was started at Bracebridge Cottages and in 1983 it became Bobby Brown's. Despite the popularity of this waterside restaurant, Bracebridge Pool is still a good place to see wild birds such as heron and moorhen.

▼ **STREETLY,** *The Entrance to Sutton Park c1965* s338003

Sutton Park is surrounded on all sides by suburbia. Sutton Coldfield itself is to the east, while Streetly borders the park to the north-west. There are several entrances to the park at Streetly, most for pedestrians only. This one gives vehicle access, but if we head north away from the road we will find ourselves in one of the finest areas of the park.

▼ **STREETLY**, *The Village c1965* s338303

Streetly is a residential community built alongside the Roman road known as Ryknild Street, traces of which can still be seen in Sutton Park. Until 1879, when a station opened on the Birmingham-Walsall railway, there had been only farmland here. Housing development followed the railway, but the station closed in 1965.

▲ **SUTTON COLDFIELD,** *Bracebridge Pool, Sutton Park c1965* S339040

Sutton Park is a National Nature Reserve, which puts it among the top rank of our protected areas. It has never been cultivated, and it is a typical example of the kind of landscape which thrived throughout the region before industrialisation. In 2001, wild Exmoor ponies were introduced to graze the coarse vegetation, keeping areas of heathland in good condition.

45

► **SUTTON COLDFIELD**
The Dorchester Suite,
Penns Hall Hotel c1965
S339121

In 1855 the Websters joined forces with James Horsfall, and the business transferred from Penns Mill to Hay Mills. It was Webster & Horsfall which made the Atlantic cables from 1858 to 1866. James Horsfall purchased Penns Hall in 1865, but in 1947 the hall was sold to Ansells; after extensive alterations, it opened as Penns Hall Hotel in 1950.

◄ **SUTTON COLDFIELD**
Penns Hall Hotel c1965 S339138

This hotel is on Penns Lane, near Walmley, south of Sutton Coldfield. The foremost stream in this area is Plants Brook, which once powered several mills. One of these was Penns Mill, operated as a wire-drawing mill by Joseph Webster from 1752. In 1759 he also took on the lease of Penns House, which became Penns Hall.

◄ **SUTTON COLDFIELD**
Penns Hall Hotel, The Interior c1965 S339141

It looks horribly dated now, but this was state-of-the-art opulence in 1965. The hotel grounds are impressive too, with woodland and the large mill pond which the Websters created to increase the power supply of Plants Brook. Stressed executives may be pleased to know there are two golf courses next to the hotel (Walmley and Pype Hayes).

SOLIHULL
AND
SUBURBS

▲ SOLIHULL
Mell Square c1966 S257022

Mell Square was begun in 1964, with the first shops opening in 1966. It was refurbished in 1987-88, so that today the foreground of this scene is occupied by a coffee bar, a traditional-style fountain and several plane trees. But the buildings are unaltered, and so are some of the tenants: Woolworth's and Marks & Spencers still occupy the two main wings of this block, as they have since 1966.

◄ SOLIHULL
Mill Lane c1966 S257072

Until 1964, Mill Lane was a picturesque street of brick and half-timbered cottages, some of them medieval. They were demolished, along with others in nearby Drury Lane, to facilitate the Mell Square development. Parts of the High Street and Warwick Road were also destroyed. This is Mill Lane today, a pedestrianised passageway from High Street to Mell Square.

▼ **SOLIHULL,** *The Civic Hall c1965* S257038

The Civic Hall was opened by the Queen in 1962 and served as a venue for social gatherings, meetings, exhibitions and amateur theatricals. Council offices and a civic suite were built alongside it after Solihull became a county borough in 1964. All were demolished in 1998 to make way for the Touchwood Centre, a shopping and leisure complex which opened in 2001.

▶ **SOLIHULL**
*Malvern Park
c1965* S257045

The Greswold family was the most distinguished in Solihull's history, and it was Humphrey Greswold who built Malvern Hall in the 18th century. It changed hands frequently until in 1926 the hall and some of its surrounding parkland were bought by Solihull Council as the nucleus for a girls' high school and a public park, to be known as Malvern Park.

▶ **SOLIHULL**
The Entrance to Malvern Hall School c1965
S257048

John Constable is known to have painted Malvern Hall at least three times - one of these paintings is now in Tate Britain. Constable was originally invited to the hall to paint a portrait of the owner, Henry Greswold Lewis, whose sister the Countess of Dysart was a friend and patron of the artist.

▶ **OLTON**
Warwick Road c1965
O52093

The coming of the railway caused semi-rural Olton to urbanise rapidly. In 1873 James Kent leased nearly 100 acres of land and started building houses for commuters. As the community expanded, so the need for shops grew; in 1883 Kent built this row on Warwick Road, rather immodestly calling it Kentish New Town.

◀ **SHIRLEY**
The Parade c1960
S337028

The vaguely Art Deco style of Shirley House (left) contrasts with the Gothic look of the Baptist church, but Stratford Road today is a much more eclectic mix than it was in the 1960s. This formless architectural jumble is set in the context of one of Birmingham's widest roads. Somehow there is room for several lanes of traffic, cycleways, pedestrian zones and even some planting.

◄ **OLTON**
*The Monastery
c1965* O52088

It is known as the Friary now, but this ornate building used to be St Bernard's Monastery. Founded by Bernard Ullathorne, the first Roman Catholic Bishop of Birmingham, it was completed in 1873. It originally served as a seminary, but only until 1889; it then became the Franciscan Monastery of the Immaculate Conception.

▲ **SHIRLEY,** *The Parade c1965* S337051

Stratford Road was first recorded in 1322, though it was just a trackway known as Shirley Street at that time. Shirley developed along it in linear fashion. This shopping parade was built for Shirley's growing commuter population in the mid 20th century, but today it is part of a seemingly endless string of commercial premises along both sides of the road.

◄ **SHIRLEY**
*The Saracen's Head and
The Parade c1965*
S337018

In 1725 a tollgate was erected across Stratford Road close to the Saracen's Head. This was the first stage on the Birmingham-London turnpike, and the Saracen's Head profited greatly from the coaches. When the railways killed the coach trade the pub remained busy, as it was also the terminus of the horse-drawn local bus service from Birmingham.

▲ **SHIRLEY**
Haslucks Green Corner c1965 S337021

This is one of the oldest parts of Shirley, where Stratford Road meets Olton Road and Haslucks Green Road. There was already a cluster of buildings here in the Elizabethan period, when Olton Road was known as Cock Lane. There was a Cock Inn on the corner then. These shops were built in the 1920s, and look much the same today.

▶ **SHIRLEY**
Stanway Road c1965 S337052

Shirley expanded hugely from the 1920s to the 1940s. Stanway Road was created in the 1930s along with several other roads in the area, and is absolutely typical of the development which took place at that time. It was originally a fordrough (a rough unmade track) across the fields of Shirley Farm, which used to be opposite the Saracen's Head.

◀ SHIRLEY
Longmore Road c1965 S337046

It is hard to imagine now, but this was still countryside not too many years ago. The name means 'long heath', and it was recorded in a deed dated 1426, now at Stratford Records Office. In the 1930s it was given over to housing development, though Longmore Farm survived until the 1950s, when it was demolished.

▼ KNOWLE
High Street c1965 K120011

Though perilously close to being engulfed by Solihull, Knowle manages to hang on to its own distinct character. Something of its former village quality remains, and it is still bordered by open countryside - something that not many towns in this county can claim. Knowle was first recorded around 1200, but its name is Saxon, so it must have been founded long before that.

▼ **KNOWLE,** *High Street c1965* K120003

The gabled, timber-framed building is Chester House, which has functioned as a library since its restoration in 1975. It is the oldest existing building on the High Street, the earliest part of it dating from around 1400. In its time it has been a farm, a carrier's business and an antique shop. It was first called Chester House in 1881.

▶ **KNOWLE**

High Street c1965 K120193

The Greswolde Hotel, or The Greswolde Arms, as it used to be, became an important coaching inn when the turnpike from Birmingham to Warwick and London opened in the 18th century. It was originally called The Mermaid, but was renamed in the early 19th century after Henry Greswolde Lewis of Malvern Hall, Solihull.

◄ **KNOWLE**
Warwick Road c1965
K120016

The shops on the left replaced a gabled, timber-framed pub, the White Swan, which was demolished in the mid 20th century, probably soon after World War II. It was a popular meeting place, with a bowling green and a quoits club. Its close neighbour, The Red Lion, is just visible on the left of this scene.

► **KNOWLE**
Guild House c1965
K120001

The timber-framed Guild House stands next to Knowle's magnificent church, and was completed in 1412. It was the home of the Guild of St Anne of Knowle (a religious and charitable foundation), but in later years it served many other purposes. In the early 20th century it was restored and given to the church.

▲ KNOWLE

The Top Lock c1965 K120008

This is the top of Knowle Locks, an impressive flight of five wide locks built in 1932 to replace six narrow ones, the remains of which can still be seen. This was part of a modernising programme undertaken in the 1930s in an unsuccessful attempt to enable the Grand Union Canal to compete with the Great Western Railway.

► DORRIDGE

The Village c1965 D102033

The railway station at the back of this picture is the reason for Dorridge's existence. Until the London to Birmingham railway was built in 1852, there was no Dorridge. In return for granting permission to the GWR to build the line across his land, local landowner George Frederick Muntz demanded the provision of a station: houses and shops inevitably followed.

▲ DORRIDGE
Dorridge Road c1960 D102005

As we leave the station, the first street we see is Dorridge Road. Broad and leafy, it retains a handful of older houses like the mock-Tudor one we can just see on the left in this photograph. The older houses are surrounded by mature trees, but later infilling has led to modern houses and bungalows with hedges of the dreaded leylandii.

◀ DORRIDGE
Manor Road c1965 D102017

The young cedar tree we see here is a splendid specimen now, with an open, spreading habit. The seat and the unnecessary fence have gone. The photograph is taken from Arden Road, which is the other side of Grange Road - all the street names have obviously been chosen to evoke a rural past which is now just a memory.

DORRIDGE, *The Village c1965* D102029

The Victorian shops on the right were among the first to be built in Dorridge, and fortunately their upper floors are largely unspoilt, though they have been re-roofed. They have acquired plastic shopfronts at ground level, and now house a tile shop, a dental practice and an Indian restaurant. The block in the background dates from the middle of the 20th century.

DORRIDGE
The Village c1965
D102031

Taken from Station Approach, looking towards the village centre, this view is much the same today. The landowner George Frederick Muntz, who gave permission for the railway, made good use of the opportunities it presented. He was responsible for building the splendid shops on the right, as well as an adjacent hotel opposite the station.

MERIDEN, *The Parish Church c1960* M153001

St Lawrence's stands on Meriden Hill, aloof from most of the community it serves, but close to a small cluster of old houses and with views towards Coventry. It is often said to have been founded by Lady Godiva, but Meriden's main claim to fame is the ancient cross on the village green reputed to mark the centre of England.

THE CITY OF COVENTRY

COVENTRY, *The Cathedral Ruins c1955* C169012

On the night of 14 November 1940, German bombs destroyed the ancient cathedral church of St Michael. It was only in 1962 that the Bishop of Coventry, in the presence of the Queen, finally consecrated the new cathedral built to replace it. The gaunt but still splendid ruins of the old building were left to stand, a lasting reminder of the folly of war.

COVENTRY, *The Choir, Holy Trinity Church c1965* C169125

A church was recorded on this site around 1113, but the oldest part of the present building dates from about 1260. Holy Trinity possesses one of the finest medieval doom paintings (depicting the Last Judgement) in Europe, painted about 1435-1460. It is currently undergoing restoration, a hugely difficult task made even harder by well-meaning 'restorers' who coated it with varnish in 1831.

COVENTRY
High Street c1955
C169010

Coventry endured dozens of air raids from 1940 to 1942, and much of the city centre was flattened. The stately buildings on the right here are among the few which survived the bombs. The National Provincial Bank (now NatWest) was built in 1931, when the High Street was widened (involving substantial demolition). Lloyd's Bank next door was built in 1932.

▶ **COVENTRY**
Broadgate c1965
C169022

In front of Broadgate's post-war development is a statue of Lady Godiva, still notorious for nudity after 1,000 years. It seems that Godiva was distressed by the taxation imposed on the citizens by her husband, Earl Leofric. He agreed to reduce the burden if she would ride naked through the streets. This she did, with her long hair strategically placed, and Leofric honoured his promise.

◀ **COVENTRY**
The Lady Godiva Clock c1965 C169026

Lady Godiva's bareback ride is a highly prized local tradition. The event is further commemorated in Broadgate by a puppet clock which dates from Coventry's post-war reconstruction. When the clock strikes the hour the doors slide open and Godiva rides once again, while Peeping Tom (a mythical figure) leers down at her from a niche in the wall above.

▲ **COVENTRY,** *Hertford Street c1955* C169006

Broadgate was always the hub around which Coventry revolved, and Hertford Street was once one of the main streets running into it, though it was constructed only in 1912. It became a major tram route from the rail station to Broadgate, but much of it was destroyed in 1940. It was redeveloped and pedestrianised in 1969.

◀**COVENTRY**
The Precinct c1965
C169020

Coventry was the first city to adopt a radical new idea: the traffic-free precinct. Construction began in 1951, and took about 5 years. The shops were built in two tiers - it is said that the architect, Donald Gibson, was inspired by the magnificent medieval Rows at Chester. Then again, perhaps this is just an urban myth!

COVENTRY
Greyfriars Green c1955
C169007

Greyfriars Green is dominated by the spire of Christchurch (c1350), all that remains of a monastery established in 1234 and demolished in 1539. The green was the site of the annual Coventry Fair until 1858. It was subject to grazing rights held by freemen until 1875, when the council turned it into permanent public space.

BLACK COUNTRY NORTH - WALSALL AND WOLVERHAMPTON

WALSALL, *The George Hotel c1965* W161028

The original George Hotel was Walsall's chief coaching inn during the era when the town was served by at least a dozen coaches daily. Its colonnaded frontage made it a distinctive and attractive building, but it was demolished in 1933, to be replaced by the hotel we see here. This was itself demolished in 1979 and replaced by shops.

◄ **WALSALL**
*St Matthew's Church
c1965* W161011

The most unusual feature of St Matthew's is an arched passageway underneath the chancel. This is a mystery for which there are various speculative explanations, some of them mundane, some more fanciful. Alfred Watkins, the man who came up with the idea of ley lines, claimed that churches were sometimes built deliberately on ancient tracks, with tunnels provided for travellers to pass through.

WALSALL, *The Approach to the Arboretum 1967* W161017

Opened in 1874, on the site of a disused quarry on the edge of the town centre, the Arboretum is a surprisingly peaceful park where fat, contented ducks loaf around a pool. Every autumn the Arboretum stages a superb display of illuminations. While not exactly rivalling Blackpool, it does bring in over a quarter of a million visitors.

▲ **CHASEWATER**
The Pleasure Park c1965 C280002

Chasewater is a large reservoir with an amusement park at its southern end, where people enjoy water sports such as sailing and water-skiing, or just paddling. The northern (Staffordshire) shore is quieter, and attracts wintering waterfowl and gulls. On a winter evening, as thousands of birds wheel across the setting sun, the Black Country can seem a long way off.

▶ **CHASEWATER**
The Pleasure Park c1965 C280004

Chasewater was built as a canal feeder in 1800; it was so efficient that its owners, Wyrley and Essington Canal Company, sold surplus water to other companies. Just after it was built, the dam gave way, pouring torrents of water across the countryside nearly as far as Tamworth. It was rebuilt and faced with stone, and remains watertight to this day.

▲ WILLENHALL
Stafford Street c1965 W238007

Willenhall has changed less than many Black Country towns, despite the impression created by this picture. It is difficult to understand how such a structure could be allowed to replace decent Victorian shops, especially in a street where many of the buildings are listed, but it was probably a source of some local pride at the time of its construction.

◀ WILLENHALL
Ye Olde Toll House c1965 W238014

One of Willenhall's more eccentric buildings, this mock-Tudor, mock-Gothic, former toll house became a restaurant in 1929 and has also been known as the Round House, though it is not really round. There used to be a smithy next door, but once the horses stopped passing through town this was taken over, logically enough, by a motor body builder.

▼ **WILLENHALL,** *St Giles's Parish Church c1965* W238013

The Reverend William Moreton was vicar here from 1795 to 1834. He was addicted to cock fighting, and had his own cockpit at the Church House. He used to preach with the church door open so as not to miss fellow cock fighters passing by on their way to matches at Darlaston Fields - and would cut short his sermon to follow them.

► **WILLENHALL**
The Memorial Park c1965
W238004

In 1849 Willenhall was stricken with cholera, and the churchyard could not accommodate all the victims. Dr Richard Wilkes gave a piece of land to take the overspill, and 211 corpses were buried there. It was made into a memorial garden in 1922. Willenhall recently won a national lottery grant to restore the park.

◄ **WEDNESFIELD**
High Street c1965
W236011

Wednesfield (like Wednesbury) takes its name from the Anglo-Saxon god Woden. The town's past industrial importance was partly based on an unpleasant speciality, the manufacture of traps. Both man and animal traps were supplied to the landed gentry, and man traps also went to the slave owners in the plantations.

► **WEDNESFIELD**
High Street c1965
W236016

In 1959 the narrow High Street still had 19th-century buildings on both sides, but an overspill housing programme was already under way and traffic was increasing. It was decided to demolish numerous properties and to rebuild them further back, thus widening the road and providing parking.

WEDNESFIELD
High Street c1965
W236015

The balustraded tower of St Thomas' church provides a nice focal point here. Originally built in 1750, it was so badly damaged by fire in 1902 that it had to be rebuilt. Locals used to say that the fire damage was so severe because the Wolverhampton fire brigade was slow to arrive - frequent stops were necessary to rest the horses.

▶ **WEDNESFIELD**

The Canal and the Flats c1965 W236013

A massive building programme changed the face of Wednesfield in the 1950s, and tower blocks like these seemed for a while to be the answer to the housing problem. The Wyrley and Essington Canal recalls an earlier development boom, when Britain was gripped by canal fever. Opened in 1797, it is now known affectionately as the Curly Wyrley.

▼ **BILSTON**

St Leonard's Parish Church 1968 B353002

A church is known to have stood on this site in the 14th century, but only the base of its tower survives. It was incorporated into this classical-style building by Francis Goodwin, which was completed in 1826. St Leonard's is actually built of brick; it was only in 1883 that it acquired its present appearance when it was cement-rendered.

▶ **BILSTON**

The Girls' High School c1965 B353013

The Girls' High School was founded in 1918 in Brueton House at Mount Pleasant, but moved to this purpose-built accommodation in Green Lanes in 1930. Brueton House now accommodates a museum and art gallery. The school became Bilston Community College in 1983.

◀ **BILSTON**
Hickman Park
c1965 B353014

The park opened in 1911 on land given by Sir Alfred Hickman, a local industrialist. He was one of several notable 19th-century ironmasters in the area. The company he founded became Bilston Steelworks, which developed into the town's largest employer. Somehow, Bilston managed to survive its closure in 1979.

▶ **TETTENHALL**
*The Parish Church
c1965* T140009

St Michael's church stands on Church Road close to Lower Green. Its predecessor was an important medieval church, but it was almost totally destroyed by fire in 1950, sad to say. Only the medieval west tower and the Victorian south porch survived. The church was rebuilt by Bernard Miller, who made no attempt to recreate the style of the original.

◀ **TETTENHALL**
Lower Green c1965
T140010

The survival of the green helps Tettenhall retain just a hint of its village character, though it is very much part of Wolverhampton now. In 910 Tettenhall was the scene of a great battle in which the Saxons under Edward the Elder and Ethelflaed (the son and daughter of Alfred the Great) decisively defeated the Danes.

▲ **TETTENHALL,** *The Post Office and Upper Green c1965* T140012

Upper Green is not so rural now, but Tettenhall remains a favoured suburb. It has always had good transport links with Wolverhampton: horse-drawn trams operated from 1878, to be replaced by trains in 1920. The station closed in 1932, but trolley buses ran instead until 1963. Today, several buses an hour still provide a link with Wolverhampton.

◄ **TETTENHALL**
The Pool, Upper Green c1965 T140002

Mock-Tudor houses are typical of the area, though these have a pleasanter outlook than most. It may be pleasant, but not necessarily peaceful, as they stand close to the A41. This was an important coaching route in the 18th and 19th centuries, part of the London to Holyhead road, which was improved by Thomas Telford in 1816.

TETTENHALL
The Pool, Upper Green
c1965 T140001

Upper Green was originally known as Marsh Green, but it has long since been drained. This pool was previously a farm pond belonging to Upper Green Farm. It opened to the public in 1934, and was intended as a children's paddling pool. The conversion was paid for by the proprietor of the Wolverhampton newspaper, the *Express and Star*.

PENN, *The Village c1965* P157024

No longer a village, but a residential suburb of Wolverhampton, Penn spreads for miles along the dual carriageway we see here. A number of attractive old cottages were demolished when the dual carriageway was created. Penn was formerly known as Upper Penn to distinguish it from nearby Lower Penn.

PENN, *St Bartholomew's Church c1965* P157029

St Bartholomew's enjoys an elevated position, possibly the site of a prehistoric fort, at the corner of Church Hill and Vicarage Road. The churchyard contains part of a Saxon preaching cross, found buried by the church in 1910. It is said to have been erected by Lady Godiva, whose son Aelfgar owned Upper Penn.

PENN
The Village c1965
P157022

The hotel on the left here is The Fox and Goose, one of several large pubs on the main road at Penn, a reminder that this has for centuries been a major line of communication. Others include The Roebuck, The Hollybush and The Rose and Crown, which used to be the terminus for a horse-drawn bus service from Wolverhampton.

PENN, *Spring Hill Corner c1965* P157026

This is one of several short parades of shops along the main road through Penn. Built in the early to mid 20th century, it remains largely unchanged today. Spring Hill Corner is an ancient junction where Springhill Lane branches off the Wolverhampton road towards Lower Penn. It runs along the top of a ridge and is prehistoric in origin.

LOWER PENN
Springhill Lane c1965
L566021

Most local placenames are Anglo-Saxon, but Penn is a Celtic name. This may indicate that it is older than other settlements in the region; or it may be that there were many other Celtic settlements, but their names were supplanted by the Anglo-Saxon ones we are familiar with today, while Penn survived unchanged.

LOWER PENN, *St Anne's Church, Springhill Lane c1965* L566020

The village of Lower Penn was once owned by Lady Godiva, and was formerly known as Nether Penn. It lies a little to the west of Penn, just across the county border in Staffordshire (where Penn also used to belong, of course). The seemingly unstoppable tide of Wolverhampton laps at its toes, but it has so far avoided being engulfed.

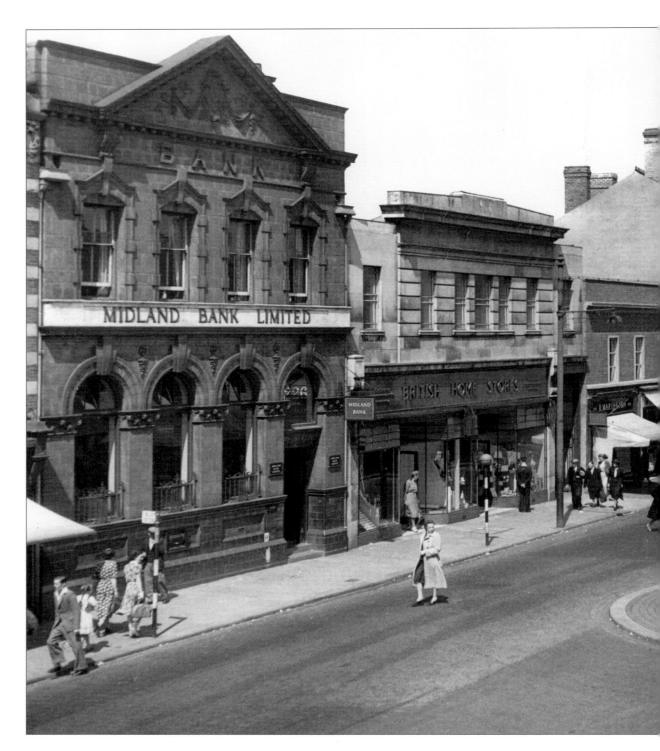

BLACK COUNTRY SOUTH - DUDLEY

DUDLEY
The Market Place c1955 D103028

The Spout is the local name for the unusually grand fountain which dominates Dudley's lively market place. It was commissioned from James Forsyth by the Earl of Dudley, and was displayed at the Paris Exhibition in 1867 before being installed in its present position. It is an exuberant affair of Italian Renaissance design, with horses, lions and some bizarre but irresistible dolphins.

▶ **DUDLEY**
The Zoo, the Gorilla c1965 D103147

The great architectural historian Nikolaus Pevsner waxed lyrical about the quality of Dudley's animal accommodation in his volume on Staffordshire, published in 1974. However, it is hard to be impressed by the sterility of this brutal-looking enclosure which houses a highly intelligent animal whose native habitat is densely vegetated.

▼ **DUDLEY**
The Entrance to Dudley Zoo c1965 D103122

This wooded hill in the town centre is topped by the ruins of a Norman castle, whose builders might not be entirely surprised to find that the outer bailey now houses a zoo: after all, exotic animals were sometimes housed in (dry) medieval moats. The zoo buildings were designed in 1936 by Tectons, the architects of London Zoo.

▶ **DUDLEY**
The Zoo, the Elephant c1965 D103255

They may have a few trees to look at, but as far as the amenities of their home are concerned, these elephants do not fare any better than the gorilla. Nor is it likely that they appreciate the chains attached to their forelegs. Attitudes to zoo conditions have changed since the 1960s, and more effort is now made to provide an acceptable environment.

◀ **WEST BROMWICH**
The Memorial Gardens c1965
W237018

West Bromwich boasts a remarkable survivor, Oak House, a magnificent 16th-century manor house. By 1894 it had fallen into disrepair. It was purchased by Reuben Farley, who paid for its restoration and presented it to the town in 1898, together with four acres of land. That land was used for the gardens illustrated in this photograph.

WEDNESBURY, *The Parish Church c1965* W235008

Wednesbury - Woden's burg - is an ancient place. Some believe that there was once a temple to the Anglo-Saxon god Woden on the hilltop site where St Bartholomew's now stands. The present church is mainly of the 15th century, and its blackened stone makes for a rather forbidding appearance. The interior, however, is full of interest - especially notable is its unusual lectern.

WEDNESBURY
The Boys' High School c1965 W235002

Known as Wood Green High School today, the former boys' school was founded in 1924 at Wood Green Lodge, on a site which is now overshadowed by the M6 motorway. It was extended in 1926 and 1932, but in 1960 the lodge was demolished and replaced with the modern wing we see here on the left.

BRIERLEY HILL, *From Amblecote Road c1965* B355001

Anybody who has ever explored the lovely countryside where Shropshire, Staffordshire and Worcestershire meet will recognise these flats, for they are visible from many rural viewpoints for miles around. Even from distant Clee Hill in Shropshire they enable you to instantly pinpoint the location of Brierley Hill.

BRIERLEY HILL
High Street 1968 B355018

The High Street looks quiet here; it usually seems much busier today. But a lot of that is just traffic passing through. There are always fewer shoppers than traders would like, and too many empty shops and charity shops. The reason is the massive shopping centre at nearby Merry Hill, opened in the 1980s on the site of a former steelworks.

▶ **BRIERLEY HILL**
The Canal Locks
c1965 B355005

This decrepit-looking lock (now expertly restored) is part of Delph Ninelocks, a spectacular piece of canal engineering on Dudley No 1 Canal. There are actually only eight locks, but there were nine when the flight was first built in 1799. Rebuilding in 1856 left the top and bottom locks intact, but replaced the remaining seven with only six new ones.

◀ **BRIERLEY HILL**
The West Midlands Constabulary c1965
B355014

Only the left-hand wing of the building is occupied by the police, while the right-hand wing is the Civic Hall. The photograph perhaps gives the impression of intimidating size and spacious grounds. In fact, this building occupies a fairly small plot in a convenient location at the end of the High Street.

▲ **KINGSWINFORD,** *The Parish Church of St Mary c1965* K84012

Above the vestry door is a superbly carved Norman tympanum showing St Michael overcoming Satan. It is thought to date from around 1120. More recently, George Woodall (1850-1925) was buried at St Mary's. He was the greatest cameo carver the world has ever known, producing an astonishing variety of delicately engraved cameo glass for Thomas Webb & Sons.

◄**KINGSWINFORD**
The Roman Catholic Church of Our Lady of Lourdes c1965 K84001

Kingswinford has an interesting Roman Catholic connection in Holbeche House, the home in 1605 of Stephen Lyttelton, a friend of Robert Catesby of Gunpowder Plot fame. The house had priest holes where Catholics could hide in times of persecution, and it was to Holbeche that the Gunpowder Plotters fled, only to be captured and killed.

KINGSWINFORD, *The Townsend Precinct c1965* K84010

The precinct is built on the site of the Townsend tram terminus, next to a junction known as the Cross, which is also the name of a good-looking pub on the opposite corner. Townsend was an early name for this part of Kingswinford, which is at one end of the High Street, and thus the 'town's end'. Trams ran to this point from both Dudley and Stourbridge from 1900 until 1926.

KINGSWINFORD
Summer Hill c1965
K84006

The four roads which meet at the Cross are Moss Grove, Market Street, High Street, and Summer Hill, which are part of the main roads linking Dudley, Kidderminster, Stourbridge and Wolverhampton. Summer Hill is to the west of the Cross, which has become the town centre since the focus of development shifted here in the 1950s.

KINGSWINFORD, *The Summerhill House Hotel c1965* K84005

Kingswinford has become a place of characterless roads, estate houses and shopping precincts, but it retains a scattering of the elegant houses built by 18th-century ironmasters and glassworks owners. Summerhill House, built in 1756, is one of these, an imposing Georgian mansion with a grand facade. It became a hotel many years ago.

◄ **WORDSLEY**
High Street c1965
W240055

The shop next to the post office used to belong to E C Whitney, a manufacturer of clerical clothing such as cassocks, surplices and stoles. Most churches in Britain were supplied by Whitney's in the early 20th century, and there was also a sizeable export market. The property is occupied by an undertaker's today, and the post office is now a dental centre.

◀ **WORDSLEY**
High Street c1965
W240052

This picture gives a tantalising glimpse of the wonderful Red House Cone, which belongs to Stuart & Sons, makers of crystal glass. Built of brick in 1790, the cone housed a central furnace around which glassmakers worked in what must have been hellish conditions. This is the only such cone to survive in the Midlands; it ceased production in 1936.

▲ **WORDSLEY,** *King George's Field c1965* W240019

The fine bay windows of this house have been filled in with concrete and adorned with graffiti, while other windows have been boarded up. Nevertheless, it is still recognisable, and part of it is still in use, though apparently not as living accommodation. It stands on the edge of King George's Field in a quiet corner of Wordsley.

◀ **WOLLASTON**
Bridgnorth Road c1965
W239012

The photographer is looking up Bridgnorth Road towards Wollaston Junction. The High Street branches left at the junction. It is unusual in being mainly residential, with commercial development centred on Bridgnorth Road. Several streets in Wollaston are named after politicians: halfway along on the right is Cobden Street, after Richard Cobden (1804-65), Liberal MP for Stockport.

WOLLASTON
The Centre c1960
W239006

The centre of Wollaston is often referred to as Wollaston Junction, recalling the time when two tram routes met here - one came from Stourbridge, and the other was the Amblecote to Kinver Light Railway. The trams ended in 1930, but buses had been running since 1914. Even today, a bus passes this traffic island every few minutes.

WOLLASTON

St James' Church c1960
W239001

Designed by Bidlake in 1860, St James' is unusually memorable for a Victorian church, mainly because it is built of blue engineering bricks. The same materials have been used for an adjacent school, the schoolmaster's house and the vicarage, and together they form a harmonious group. Modern buildings have been added, but at least a vague effort has been made to blend them in.

WOLLASTON, *Kingsway House, The Farm Estate c1960* W239008

The name gives the game away - not so long ago it was farmland, and now it is a housing estate. Horses grazing peacefully in a paddock act as a reminder of that rural past, and the Stourbridge Canal and the Staffordshire countryside are just a stone's throw away. Many of the residents must enjoy excellent views, because this is an unusually hilly estate.

WOLLASTON
High Park Avenue
c1955 W239004

Just 100 years ago Wollaston was a rural community. That began to change in the first half of the 20th century, but it was only after 1950 that the real housing boom began, resulting in massive residential estates. High Park Avenue and High Park Estate are named after the farm they supplanted, previously one of the largest in the district.

WOLLASTON, *High Park Avenue c1960* W239003

John Darby of High Park Farm operated a substantial milk delivery service, using a horse-drawn float. That finished when the farm closed, but the Darbys are still around - Graham Darby is currently licensee of The Gate Hangs Well on High Park Avenue. There is another High Park Farm too, just across the Staffordshire border.

STOURBRIDGE

High Street c1950 S213033

Smarts occupies part of a block known as Bordeaux House, so named because when it was built in 1894 it was the home of a wine importer, Rutlands. It is now occupied by a catalogue bargain shop and a building society, and the clock has gone. The buildings on the left were demolished to make way for a MacDonald's restaurant in 1988.

STOURBRIDGE

High Street c1950 S213010

Until 1974 Stourbridge was in Worcestershire, and was always considered slightly posher than its Staffordshire neighbours. It was right on the edge of the Black Country, and it had almost the air of a rural market town. This picture gives some idea of the quality and variety of the buildings which lined the High Street in the 1950s.

▶ **STOURBRIDGE**
High Street c1950
S213012

Stourbridge's great tragedy is its ring road, one of the most damaging examples of its type in existence. It throttles the town centre, and its construction involved the wholesale demolition of attractive buildings. Those on the right of this picture were lucky: they narrowly escaped demolition. But they have still suffered the indignity of inappropriate modernisation.

◀ **STOURBRIDGE**
High Street and the Public Library c1950
S213011

All the buildings in the foreground were demolished for the ring road. The library survives, but it is cut off from High Street by the ring road. It was built in 1905 with the help of a £3,000 donation from the American philanthropist Andrew Carnegie. The library has since moved to another site, and this building is now used by Stourbridge College.

▲ **STOURBRIDGE,** *The Mitre Inn c1950* S213006

The original Mitre Inn was demolished to make way for the widening of Crown Lane, which is on the left in this photograph. The 'new' Mitre Inn looks much the same today as it did in 1955. It is worth a close look to appreciate the carvings on the beams and the grapevine design on the square drainpipes.

◀ **STOURBRIDGE**
High Street from The Mitre Inn c1965 S213167

The clock is a focal point of the town. Its column was cast at Stourbridge Ironworks (just a short walk away, by the canal) in 1857. The lovely building with Dutch gables (left) is a wine merchant's established in 1797, Nickolls & Perks Ltd. Formerly the Board Inn, it is possibly the oldest commercial building in Stourbridge.

STOURBRIDGE, *The Town Hall and Market Street c1960* S213036

Designed by Thomas Robinson and completed in 1887, the red-brick town hall deserves a more spacious and prominent setting than Market Street. In the 1980s it was cleaned and renovated and partially incorporated within the Crown Centre shopping complex. Access to the town hall is from the shopping centre, which was built onto the rear of it.

STOURBRIDGE
Hagley Road c1950
S213032

Two car dealerships feature in this scene - Stour Valley Motors selling Austins (centre right), and just beyond it, a Ford dealer. Both these fine buildings were demolished to make way for modern showrooms and forecourt sales areas. The Ford dealership is now Quicks, but Stour Valley is still trading under the same name.

STOURBRIDGE, *The Broadway Stores c1965* S213081

Broadway Stores is in Norton, where a large housing estate extends right to the county border. The stores is Broadway Service Station now, with a modern forecourt. Just across the road is the Gigmill pub, a reminder of Stourbridge's days as a wool town in the 17th century. A gig was a machine which raised the nap on cloth.

▼ **OLD SWINFORD,** *Hagley Road c1955* O51015

Old Swinford is a suburb of Stourbridge today, which represents a reversal of fortune: the Domesday Book (1086) recorded Stourbridge as part of the manor of 'Suineford'. The scene recorded in this photograph is impossible to find today, so greatly has Hagley Road changed. The charming cottages on the left have either been demolished or modernised out of recognition.

▶ **OLD SWINFORD**
Hagley Road c1960
O51001

This photograph shows a similar view to O51014, but much has changed in the intervening five years. Look at the depressing differences in the first building on the left, which has gained a coat of cement render and lost its original windows. The three ugly new traffic signs and modern street lights are also a sign of the times.

◄ OLD SWINFORD
Hagley Road c1955
O51014

The photographer was standing towards the northern end of Hagley Road, looking towards Stourbridge. The view is greatly changed today, with the cottages on the left barely recognisable. On the right-hand side of the road a solitary petrol pump is just visible outside the white-painted garage. A modern petrol station stands there now.

► OLD SWINFORD
The Castle,
Church Road c1960 O51003

There are few places in the Black Country as attractive as this secluded corner of Old Swinford, where superb Georgian houses grace quiet streets below a medieval church. There are a few oddities too, such as this charming building with its mix of brick, stone and timber-framing. Despite its name, it was never a castle, but parts of it are 15th-century.

OLD SWINFORD, *The Labour in Vain c1955* O51013

Red Hill is one of the pleasantest streets in Stourbridge, created centuries ago by cutting through the red sandstone which outcrops locally. At the bottom of the hill stands this fine pub, still looking much as it did in 1955. One thing has changed - the unpleasant sign which depicted two white women scrubbing a black man has been removed.

INDEX

Frith Book Co Titles

www.francisfrith.co.uk

The Frith Book Company publishes over 100 new titles each year. A selection of those currently available as listed below. For latest catalogue please contact Frith Book Co.
Town Books 96 pages, approximately 100 photos. **County and Themed Books** 128 pages, approximately 150 photos (unless specified). All titles hardback with laminated case and jacket, except those indicated pb (paperback)

Amersham, Chesham & Rickmansworth (pb)	1-85937-340-2	£9.99	Devon (pb)	1-85937-297-x	£9.99
Andover (pb)	1-85937-292-9	£9.99	Devon Churches (pb)	1-85937-250-3	£9.99
Aylesbury (pb)	1-85937-227-9	£9.99	Dorchester (pb)	1-85937-307-0	£9.99
Barnstaple (pb)	1-85937-300-3	£9.99	Dorset (pb)	1-85937-269-4	£9.99
Basildon Living Memories (pb)	1-85937-515-4	£9.99	Dorset Coast (pb)	1-85937-299-6	£9.99
Bath (pb)	1-85937-419-0	£9.99	Dorset Living Memories (pb)	1-85937-584-7	£9.99
Bedford (pb)	1-85937-205-8	£9.99	Down the Severn (pb)	1-85937-560-x	£9.99
Bedfordshire Living Memories	1-85937-513-8	£14.99	Down The Thames (pb)	1-85937-278-3	£9.99
Belfast (pb)	1-85937-303-8	£9.99	Down the Trent	1-85937-311-9	£14.99
Berkshire (pb)	1-85937-191-4	£9.99	East Anglia (pb)	1-85937-265-1	£9.99
Berkshire Churches	1-85937-170-1	£17.99	East Grinstead (pb)	1-85937-138-8	£9.99
Berkshire Living Memories	1-85937-332-1	£14.99	East London	1-85937-080-2	£14.99
Black Country	1-85937-497-2	£12.99	East Sussex (pb)	1-85937-606-1	£9.99
Blackpool (pb)	1-85937-393-3	£9.99	Eastbourne (pb)	1-85937-399-2	£9.99
Bognor Regis (pb)	1-85937-431-x	£9.99	Edinburgh (pb)	1-85937-193-0	£8.99
Bournemouth (pb)	1-85937-545-6	£9.99	England In The 1880s	1-85937-331-3	£17.99
Bradford (pb)	1-85937-204-x	£9.99	Essex - Second Selection	1-85937-456-5	£14.99
Bridgend (pb)	1-85937-386-0	£7.99	Essex (pb)	1-85937-270-8	£9.99
Bridgwater (pb)	1-85937-305-4	£9.99	Essex Coast	1-85937-342-9	£14.99
Bridport (pb)	1-85937-327-5	£9.99	Essex Living Memories	1-85937-490-5	£14.99
Brighton (pb)	1-85937-192-2	£8.99	Exeter	1-85937-539-1	£9.99
Bristol (pb)	1-85937-264-3	£9.99	Exmoor (pb)	1-85937-608-8	£9.99
British Life A Century Ago (pb)	1-85937-213-9	£9.99	Falmouth (pb)	1-85937-594-4	£9.99
Buckinghamshire (pb)	1-85937-200-7	£9.99	Folkestone (pb)	1-85937-124-8	£9.99
Camberley (pb)	1-85937-222-8	£9.99	Frome (pb)	1-85937-317-8	£9.99
Cambridge (pb)	1-85937-422-0	£9.99	Glamorgan	1-85937-488-3	£14.99
Cambridgeshire (pb)	1-85937-420-4	£9.99	Glasgow (pb)	1-85937-190-6	£9.99
Cambridgeshire Villages	1-85937-523-5	£14.99	Glastonbury (pb)	1-85937-338-0	£7.99
Canals And Waterways (pb)	1-85937-291-0	£9.99	Gloucester (pb)	1-85937-232-5	£9.99
Canterbury Cathedral (pb)	1-85937-179-5	£9.99	Gloucestershire (pb)	1-85937-561-8	£9.99
Cardiff (pb)	1-85937-093-4	£9.99	Great Yarmouth (pb)	1-85937-426-3	£9.99
Carmarthenshire (pb)	1-85937-604-5	£9.99	Greater Manchester (pb)	1-85937-266-x	£9.99
Chelmsford (pb)	1-85937-310-0	£9.99	Guildford (pb)	1-85937-410-7	£9.99
Cheltenham (pb)	1-85937-095-0	£9.99	Hampshire (pb)	1-85937-279-1	£9.99
Cheshire (pb)	1-85937-271-6	£9.99	Harrogate (pb)	1-85937-423-9	£9.99
Chester (pb)	1-85937-382 8	£9.99	Hastings and Bexhill (pb)	1-85937-131-0	£9.99
Chesterfield (pb)	1-85937-378-x	£9.99	Heart of Lancashire (pb)	1-85937-197-3	£9.99
Chichester (pb)	1-85937-228-7	£9.99	Helston (pb)	1-85937-214-7	£9.99
Churches of East Cornwall (pb)	1-85937-249-x	£9.99	Hereford (pb)	1-85937-175-2	£9.99
Churches of Hampshire (pb)	1-85937-207-4	£9.99	Herefordshire (pb)	1-85937-567-7	£9.99
Cinque Ports & Two Ancient Towns	1-85937-492-1	£14.99	Herefordshire Living Memories	1-85937-514-6	£14.99
Colchester (pb)	1-85937-188-4	£8.99	Hertfordshire (pb)	1-85937-247-3	£9.99
Cornwall (pb)	1-85937-229-5	£9.99	Horsham (pb)	1-85937-432-8	£9.99
Cornwall Living Memories	1-85937-248-1	£14.99	Humberside (pb)	1-85937-605-3	£9.99
Cotswolds (pb)	1-85937-230-9	£9.99	Hythe, Romney Marsh, Ashford (pb)	1-85937-256-2	£9.99
Cotswolds Living Memories	1-85937-255-4	£14.99	Ipswich (pb)	1-85937-424-7	£9.99
County Durham (pb)	1-85937-398-4	£9.99	Isle of Man (pb)	1-85937-268-6	£9.99
Croydon Living Memories (pb)	1-85937-162-0	£9.99	Isle of Wight (pb)	1-85937-429-8	£9.99
Cumbria (pb)	1-85937-621-5	£9.99	Isle of Wight Living Memories	1-85937-304-6	£14.99
Derby (pb)	1-85937-367-4	£9.99	Kent (pb)	1-85937-189-2	£9.99
Derbyshire (pb)	1-85937-196-5	£9.99	Kent Living Memories(pb)	1-85937-401-8	£9.99
Derbyshire Living Memories	1-85937-330-5	£14.99	Kings Lynn (pb)	1-85937-334-8	£9.99

Available from your local bookshop or from the publisher

Frith Book Co Titles (continued)

Lake District (pb)	1-85937-275-9	£9.99	Sherborne (pb)	1-85937-301-1	£9.99
Lancashire Living Memories	1-85937-335-6	£14.99	Shrewsbury (pb)	1-85937-325-9	£9.99
Lancaster, Morecambe, Heysham (pb)	1-85937-233-3	£9.99	Shropshire (pb)	1-85937-326-7	£9.99
Leeds (pb)	1-85937-202-3	£9.99	Shropshire Living Memories	1-85937-643-6	£14.99
Leicester (pb)	1-85937-381-x	£9.99	Somerset	1-85937-153-1	£14.99
Leicestershire & Rutland Living Memories	1-85937-500-6	£12.99	South Devon Coast	1-85937-107-8	£14.99
Leicestershire (pb)	1-85937-185-x	£9.99	South Devon Living Memories (pb)	1-85937-609-6	£9.99
Lighthouses	1-85937-257-0	£9.99	South East London (pb)	1-85937-263-5	£9.99
Lincoln (pb)	1-85937-380-1	£9.99	South Somerset	1-85937-318-6	£14.99
Lincolnshire (pb)	1-85937-433-6	£9.99	South Wales	1-85937-519-7	£14.99
Liverpool and Merseyside (pb)	1-85937-234-1	£9.99	Southampton (pb)	1-85937-427-1	£9.99
London (pb)	1-85937-183-3	£9.99	Southend (pb)	1-85937-313-5	£9.99
London Living Memories	1-85937-454-9	£14.99	Southport (pb)	1-85937-425-5	£9.99
Ludlow (pb)	1-85937-176-0	£9.99	St Albans (pb)	1-85937-341-0	£9.99
Luton (pb)	1-85937-235-x	£9.99	St Ives (pb)	1-85937-415-8	£9.99
Maidenhead (pb)	1-85937-339-9	£9.99	Stafford Living Memories (pb)	1-85937-503-0	£9.99
Maidstone (pb)	1-85937-391-7	£9.99	Staffordshire (pb)	1-85937-308-9	£9.99
Manchester (pb)	1-85937-198-1	£9.99	Stourbridge (pb)	1-85937-530-8	£9.99
Marlborough (pb)	1-85937-336-4	£9.99	Stratford upon Avon (pb)	1-85937-388-7	£9.99
Middlesex	1-85937-158-2	£14.99	Suffolk (pb)	1-85937-221-x	£9.99
Monmouthshire	1-85937-532-4	£14.99	Suffolk Coast (pb)	1-85937-610-x	£9.99
New Forest (pb)	1-85937-390-9	£9.99	Surrey (pb)	1-85937-240-6	£9.99
Newark (pb)	1-85937-366-6	£9.99	Surrey Living Memories	1-85937-328-3	£14.99
Newport, Wales (pb)	1-85937-258-9	£9.99	Sussex (pb)	1-85937-184-1	£9.99
Newquay (pb)	1-85937-421-2	£9.99	Sutton (pb)	1-85937-337-2	£9.99
Norfolk (pb)	1-85937-195-7	£9.99	Swansea (pb)	1-85937-167-1	£9.99
Norfolk Broads	1-85937-486-7	£14.99	Taunton (pb)	1-85937-314-3	£9.99
Norfolk Living Memories (pb)	1-85937-402-6	£9.99	Tees Valley & Cleveland (pb)	1-85937-623-1	£9.99
North Buckinghamshire	1-85937-626-6	£14.99	Teignmouth (pb)	1-85937-370-4	£7.99
North Devon Living Memories	1-85937-261-9	£14.99	Thanet (pb)	1-85937-116-7	£9.99
North Hertfordshire	1-85937-547-2	£14.99	Tiverton (pb)	1-85937-178-7	£9.99
North London (pb)	1-85937-403-4	£9.99	Torbay (pb)	1-85937-597-9	£9.99
North Somerset	1-85937-302-x	£14.99	Truro (pb)	1-85937-598-7	£9.99
North Wales (pb)	1-85937-298-8	£9.99	Victorian & Edwardian Dorset	1-85937-254-6	£14.99
North Yorkshire (pb)	1-85937-236-8	£9.99	Victorian & Edwardian Kent (pb)	1-85937-624-X	£9.99
Northamptonshire Living Memories	1-85937-529-4	£14.99	Victorian & Edwardian Maritime Album (pb)	1-85937-622-3	£9.99
Northamptonshire	1-85937-150-7	£14.99	Victorian and Edwardian Sussex (pb)	1-85937-625-8	£9.99
Northumberland Tyne & Wear (pb)	1-85937-281-3	£9.99	Villages of Devon (pb)	1-85937-293-7	£9.99
Northumberland	1-85937-522-7	£14.99	Villages of Kent (pb)	1-85937-294-5	£9.99
Norwich (pb)	1-85937-194-9	£8.99	Villages of Sussex (pb)	1-85937-295-3	£9.99
Nottingham (pb)	1-85937-324-0	£9.99	Warrington (pb)	1-85937-507-3	£9.99
Nottinghamshire (pb)	1-85937-187-6	£9.99	Warwick (pb)	1-85937-518-9	£9.99
Oxford (pb)	1-85937-411-5	£9.99	Warwickshire (pb)	1-85937-203-1	£9.99
Oxfordshire (pb)	1-85937-430-1	£9.99	Welsh Castles (pb)	1-85937-322-4	£9.99
Oxfordshire Living Memories	1-85937-525-1	£14.99	West Midlands (pb)	1-85937-289-9	£9.99
Paignton (pb)	1-85937-374-7	£7.99	West Sussex (pb)	1-85937-607-x	£9.99
Peak District (pb)	1-85937-280-5	£9.99	West Yorkshire (pb)	1-85937-201-5	£9.99
Pembrokeshire	1-85937-262-7	£14.99	Weston Super Mare (pb)	1-85937-306-2	£9.99
Penzance (pb)	1-85937-595-2	£9.99	Weymouth (pb)	1-85937-209-0	£9.99
Peterborough (pb)	1-85937-219-8	£9.99	Wiltshire (pb)	1-85937-277-5	£9.99
Picturesque Harbours	1-85937-208-2	£14.99	Wiltshire Churches (pb)	1-85937-171-x	£9.99
Piers	1-85937-237-6	£17.99	Wiltshire Living Memories (pb)	1-85937-396-8	£9.99
Plymouth (pb)	1-85937-389-5	£9.99	Winchester (pb)	1-85937-428-x	£9.99
Poole & Sandbanks (pb)	1-85937-251-1	£9.99	Windsor (pb)	1-85937-333-x	£9.99
Preston (pb)	1-85937-212-0	£9.99	Wokingham & Bracknell (pb)	1-85937-329-1	£9.99
Reading (pb)	1-85937-238-4	£9.99	Woodbridge (pb)	1-85937-498-0	£9.99
Redhill to Reigate (pb)	1-85937-596-0	£9.99	Worcester (pb)	1-85937-165-5	£9.99
Ringwood (pb)	1-85937-384-4	£7.99	Worcestershire Living Memories	1-85937-489-1	£14.99
Romford (pb)	1-85937-319-4	£9.99	Worcestershire	1-85937-152-3	£14.99
Royal Tunbridge Wells (pb)	1-85937-504-9	£9.99	York (pb)	1-85937-199-x	£9.99
Salisbury (pb)	1-85937-239-2	£9.99	Yorkshire (pb)	1-85937-186-8	£9.99
Scarborough (pb)	1-85937-379-8	£9.99	Yorkshire Coastal Memories	1-85937-506-5	£14.99
Sevenoaks and Tonbridge (pb)	1-85937-392-5	£9.99	Yorkshire Dales	1-85937-502-2	£14.99
Sheffield & South Yorks (pb)	1-85937-267-8	£9.99	Yorkshire Living Memories (pb)	1-85937-397-6	£9.99

See Frith books on the internet at www.francisfrith.co.uk

FRITH PRODUCTS & SERVICES

Francis Frith would doubtless be pleased to know that the pioneering publishing venture he started in 1860 still continues today. Over a hundred and forty years later, The Francis Frith Collection continues in the same innovative tradition and is now one of the foremost publishers of vintage photographs in the world. Some of the current activities include:

Interior Decoration

Today Frith's photographs can be seen framed and as giant wall murals in thousands of pubs, restaurants, hotels, banks, retail stores and other public buildings throughout the country. In every case they enhance the unique local atmosphere of the places they depict and provide reminders of gentler days in an increasingly busy and frenetic world.

Product Promotions

Frith products are used by many major companies to promote the sales of their own products or to reinforce their own history and heritage. Frith promotions have been used by Hovis bread, Courage beers, Scots Porage Oats, Colman's mustard, Cadbury's foods, Mellow Birds coffee, Dunhill pipe tobacco, Guinness, and Bulmer's Cider.

Genealogy and Family History

As the interest in family history and roots grows world-wide, more and more people are turning to Frith's photographs of Great Britain for images of the towns, villages and streets where their ancestors lived; and, of course, photographs of the churches and chapels where their ancestors were christened, married and buried are an essential part of every genealogy tree and family album.

Frith Products

All Frith photographs are available Framed or just as Mounted Prints and Posters (size 23 x 16 inches). These may be ordered from the address below. From time to time other products - Address Books, Calendars, Table Mats, etc - are available.

The Internet

Already fifty thousand Frith photographs can be viewed and purchased on the internet through the Frith websites and a myriad of partner sites.

For more detailed information on Frith companies and products, look at these sites:

www.francisfrith.co.uk
www.francisfrith.com
(for North American visitors)

See the complete list of Frith Books at:

www.francisfrith.co.uk

This web site is regularly updated with the latest list of publications from the Frith Book Company. If you wish to buy books relating to another part of the country that your local bookshop does not stock, you may purchase on-line.

For further information, trade, or author enquiries please contact us at the address below:
The Francis Frith Collection, Frith's Barn, Teffont, Salisbury, Wiltshire, England SP3 5QP.
Tel: +44 (0)1722 716 376 Fax: +44 (0)1722 716 881 Email: sales@francisfrith.co.uk

See Frith books on the internet at www.francisfrith.co.uk

FREE MOUNTED PRINT

Mounted Print
Overall size 14 x 11 inches

Fill in and cut out this voucher and return
it with your remittance for £2.25 (to cover postage and handling). Offer valid for delivery to UK addresses only.

Choose any photograph included in this book.
Your SEPIA print will be A4 in size. It will be mounted in a cream mount with a burgundy rule line (overall size 14 x 11 inches).

Order additional Mounted Prints at HALF PRICE (only £7.49 each*)
If you would like to order more Frith prints from this book, possibly as gifts for friends and family, you can buy them at half price (with no additional postage and handling costs).

Have your Mounted Prints framed
For an extra £14.95 per print* you can have your mounted print(s) framed in an elegant polished wood and gilt moulding, overall size 16 x 13 inches (no additional postage and handling required).

---

* IMPORTANT!

These special prices are only available if you order at the same time as you order your free mounted print. You must use the ORIGINAL VOUCHER on this page (no copies permitted). We can only despatch to one address.

Send completed Voucher form to:
The Francis Frith Collection, Frith's Barn, Teffont, Salisbury, Wiltshire SP3 5QP

CHOOSE ANY IMAGE FROM THIS BOOK

Voucher for **FREE** and Reduced Price Frith Prints

Please do not photocopy this voucher. Only the original is valid, so please fill it in, cut it out and return it to us with your order.

Picture ref no	Page no	Qty	Mounted @ £7.49	Framed + £14.95	Total Cost
		1	Free of charge*	£	£
			£7.49	£	£
			£7.49	£	£
			£7.49	£	£
			£7.49	£	£
			£7.49	£	£
Please allow 28 days for delivery			* Post & handling (UK)		£2.25
			Total Order Cost		£

Title of this book . . . .

I enclose a cheque/postal order for £ . . . .

made payable to 'The Francis Frith Collection'

OR please debit my Mastercard / Visa / Switch / Amex card

(credit cards please on all overseas orders), details below

Card Number

Issue No (Switch only)   Valid from (Amex/Switch)

Expires   Signature

Name Mr/Mrs/Ms . . . .

Address . . . .

. . . .

. . . .

. . . . Postcode . . . .

Daytime Tel No . . . .

Email . . . .

Valid to 31/12/05

Would you like to find out more about Francis Frith?

We have recently recruited some entertaining speakers who are happy to visit local groups, clubs and societies to give an illustrated talk documenting Frith's travels and photographs. If you are a member of such a group and are interested in hosting a presentation, we would love to hear from you.

Our speakers bring with them a small selection of our local town and county books, together with sample prints. They are happy to take orders. A small proportion of the order value is donated to the group who have hosted the presentation. The talks are therefore an excellent way of fundraising for small groups and societies.

Can you help us with information about any of the Frith photographs in this book?

We are gradually compiling an historical record for each of the photographs in the Frith archive. It is always fascinating to find out the names of the people shown in the pictures, as well as insights into the shops, buildings and other features depicted.

If you recognize anyone in the photographs in this book, or if you have information not already included in the author's caption, do let us know. We would love to hear from you, and will try to publish it in future books or articles.

Our production team

Frith books are produced by a small dedicated team at offices in the converted Grade II listed 18th-century barn at Teffont near Salisbury, illustrated above. Most have worked with the Frith Collection for many years. All have in common one quality: they have a passion for the Frith Collection. The team is constantly expanding, but currently includes:

Jason Buck, John Buck, Douglas Mitchell-Burns, Ruth Butler, Heather Crisp, Isobel Hall, Julian Hight, Peter Horne, James Kinnear, Karen Kinnear, Tina Leary, David Marsh, Sue Molloy, Kate Rotondetto, Dean Scource, Eliza Sackett, Terence Sackett, Sandra Sampson, Adrian Sanders, Sandra Sanger, Julia Skinner, Lewis Taylor, Shelley Tolcher and Lorraine Tuck.